First World War
and Army of Occupation
War Diary
France, Belgium and Germany

19 DIVISION
56 Infantry Brigade
King's (Shropshire Light Infantry)
1/4th Battalion
5 January 1918 - 18 May 1919

WO95/2078/2

The Naval & Military Press Ltd
www.nmarchive.com
Published in association with The National Archives

Published by

The Naval & Military Press Ltd

Unit 10 Ridgewood Industrial Park,

Uckfield, East Sussex,

TN22 5QE England

Tel: +44 (0) 1825 749494

www.naval-military-press.com

www.nmarchive.com

This diary has been reprinted in facsimile from the original. Any imperfections are inevitably reproduced and the quality may fall short of modern type and cartographic standards.

© **Crown Copyright**
Images reproduced by permission of The National Archives, London, England, 2015.

Contents

Document type	Place/Title	Date From	Date To
Heading	WO95/2078/2		
Heading	4th Bn K.S.L.I. Feb 1918-May 1919 from 63 Div. 190 Brigade		
Heading	War Diary of 1/4th Battalion The King's (Shropshire Light Infantry). From 1st, February, 1918 To 28th February, 1918		
War Diary	Beaulencourt	01/02/1918	03/02/1918
War Diary	Lechelle	04/02/1918	04/02/1918
War Diary	Welsh Ridge	05/01/1918	06/01/1918
War Diary	Wood Trench	11/02/1918	11/02/1918
War Diary	Baraste	14/02/1918	21/02/1918
War Diary	Bouzincourt	22/02/1918	28/02/1918
Heading	4th Battalion King's Shropshire Light Infantry March 1918		
War Diary	Bouzincourt	01/03/1918	07/03/1918
War Diary	Beaulencourt	07/03/1918	21/03/1918
War Diary	Sanders Camp	21/03/1918	31/03/1918
Heading	1/4th Battalion King's Shropshire Light Infantry April 1918		
War Diary	Wulverghem	01/04/1918	10/04/1918
War Diary	Hill 63	11/04/1918	11/04/1918
War Diary	Army Line	12/04/1918	15/04/1918
War Diary	Rossignol Camp	15/04/1918	16/04/1918
War Diary	N.20 A B.	17/04/1918	19/04/1918
War Diary	Wippenhoek	20/04/1918	21/04/1918
War Diary	Tunnellers Camp	22/04/1918	25/04/1918
War Diary	Ouderdom	26/04/1918	01/05/1918
War Diary	Dickebush	02/05/1918	04/05/1918
War Diary	N. Busseboom	05/05/1918	05/05/1918
War Diary	L13 b. (S.128)	06/05/1918	09/05/1918
War Diary	NE Of Dickebusch	11/05/1918	12/05/1918
War Diary	L 136	13/05/1918	17/05/1918
War Diary	Omey	18/05/1918	28/05/1918
War Diary	N.W. Chaumuzy	29/05/1918	29/05/1918
War Diary	Chambrecy	29/05/1918	29/05/1918
War Diary	E of Bouzouse	30/05/1918	31/05/1918
War Diary	Bridge E Of Bligny	01/06/1918	04/06/1918
War Diary	Chaumuzy	05/06/1918	06/06/1918
War Diary	Bois de Courton	07/06/1918	10/06/1918
War Diary	NW Chaumuzy	11/06/1918	18/06/1918
War Diary	Hautvillers Wood	19/06/1918	19/06/1918
War Diary	Le. Mesnil	20/06/1918	20/06/1918
War Diary	Oyes	21/06/1918	23/06/1918
War Diary	Broussy Le Petit	24/06/1918	30/06/1918
War Diary	Bauesy La Petit	01/07/1918	02/07/1918
War Diary	Auldnay and Planches	03/07/1918	03/07/1918
War Diary	Azincourt	04/07/1918	06/07/1918
War Diary	Vercouch	07/07/1918	13/07/1918
War Diary	Lieres	14/07/1918	06/08/1918
War Diary	La Bassee Canal 59 36 A SE	07/08/1918	10/08/1918

War Diary	Locon	11/08/1918	17/08/1918
War Diary	Annezin	18/08/1918	31/08/1918
War Diary	Chocques	01/09/1918	04/09/1918
War Diary	Le Touret	05/09/1918	08/09/1918
War Diary	E Bois Biez	09/09/1918	16/09/1918
War Diary	Locon	17/09/1918	21/09/1918
War Diary	Criceth	21/09/1918	30/09/1918
War Diary	Lacoutre	01/10/1918	03/10/1918
War Diary	Chamblain Chatelain	04/10/1918	04/10/1918
War Diary	Bavincourt	05/10/1918	07/10/1918
War Diary	Graincourt	07/10/1918	09/10/1918
War Diary	Proville	10/10/1918	12/10/1918
War Diary	Cambrai	13/10/1918	17/10/1918
War Diary	Avesnes Lez Aubert	18/10/1918	20/10/1918
War Diary	St. Albert	21/10/1918	23/10/1918
War Diary	Cagnoncles	24/10/1918	24/10/1918
War Diary	St. Albert	25/10/1918	26/10/1918
War Diary	Cagnoncles	27/10/1918	01/11/1918
War Diary	Vendegies	02/11/1918	03/11/1918
War Diary	Jenlain	04/11/1918	04/11/1918
War Diary	Wargnies Le-Grand	05/11/1918	05/11/1918
War Diary	La Flamengrie	06/11/1918	06/11/1918
War Diary	Bry	07/11/1918	08/11/1918
War Diary	Taisnieres	09/11/1918	09/11/1918
War Diary	Laisnieres	10/11/1918	10/11/1918
War Diary	Houdain	10/11/1918	10/11/1918
War Diary	Bry	11/11/1918	13/11/1918
War Diary	Vendigies	14/11/1918	14/11/1918
War Diary	Rieux	15/11/1918	24/11/1918
War Diary	Cambrai	25/11/1918	28/11/1918
War Diary	Rubempre	29/11/1918	13/12/1918
War Diary	Fieffes & Montrelet	14/12/1918	14/12/1918
War Diary	Villers L'Hopital	15/12/1918	14/05/1919
War Diary	Havre	15/05/1919	15/05/1919
War Diary	Harfleur	16/05/1919	18/05/1919

woods/2018 (2)
9:30am

woods/2018 (2)
9:30am

19TH DIVISION
56TH INFY. BDE

4TH BN K.S.L.I.
FEB 1918-MAY 1919

from 63 DIV.
190 Brigade

19TH DIVISION
56TH INFY. BDE

Headquarters,
4th Bn. The King's (Shropshire L.I.)

28th February, 1918.

WAR DIARY

of

1/4TH BATTALION THE KING'S (SHROPSHIRE LIGHT INFANTRY).

From 1st February, 1918.
To   28th February, 1918.

A B Garrett
Lieut. Colonel.
Commdg. 1/4th Bn. The King's (Shropshire Light Infantry).

TO
Officer i/c A.G's. Office, Base.

WAR DIARY or **INTELLIGENCE SUMMARY.**
(Erase heading not required.)

Army Form C. 2118.

4th Kings Shropshire LI

Place	Date	Hour	Summary of Events and Information	Remarks and references to Appendices
BEAULEN- -COURT	1st		In camp reorganizing Battn. the 63rd Division being in Corps Reserve	a24
"	3rd		Read Orders that Battn. would be transferred to 19th Div. on 4th	a24
LECHELLE	4th		Battn. to PIONEER CAMP & joined 56th Brigade in 19th Division	a24
"			Draft of 2 Officers & 107 O.R. from 3rd K.S.L.I. joined	a24
WELSHRIDGE	5th		Battn. took over LEFT CENTRE Section from 9th R.Welsh, proceeding by Light Rly to TRESCAULT & thence by march route via BEAUCAMP.	a24
"	6th		Nine Officers (3rd Lieuts) joined	a24
WOOD TRENCH	11th		Battn. relieved by 9th R.W. & moved into Serpent Trenches 5 Officers & 1200 O.R. and from Div. Wing at Base at LECHELLE	a24
BARASTE	14th/15th		Battn. relieved by Hawke Battn. & moved by march route to TRESCAULT & thence by Light Rly to ROCQUINY & march to BARASTE arry 3 a.m. on 15th	a24
"	15-21st		In camp, reorganizing & receiving new drafts to conform	a24
BOUZINCOURT	22nd		Battn. (& 56th Brigade) march to ROCQUINEY thence by railway to ALBERT & march to Billets arrg at 6 p.m.	a24
			contd	

Army Form C. 2118.

WAR DIARY
or
INTELLIGENCE SUMMARY.
(Erase heading not required.)

4th Kings Shropshire L.I.

Place	Date	Hour	Summary of Events and Information	Remarks and references to Appendices
BOUZIN- -COURT	23rd to 28th		February 1918	
			Battn in Billets, training and reorganizing of Companies & Platoons	
			Strength 18th — 150 O.R. joined on 18th	A.1.9
			1 Officer + 70 O.R. " 20th	A.1.9
			Battle Casualties during Month O.R. 1 killed + wounded 6ns	A.1.9

A.R. Farrett Lt Col
Comdg 4th Kings Shropshire L.I.

19th Division.
56th Infantry Brigade.

WAR DIARY

4th BATTALION

KING'S SHROPSHIRE LIGHT INFANTRY

MARCH 1918

Army Form C. 2118.

56/19

4 Kings Shropshire L.I.

WAR DIARY
or
INTELLIGENCE SUMMARY.
(Erase heading not required.)

Place	Date	Hour	Summary of Events and Information	Remarks and references to Appendices
BOUZIN-COURT	1st	7pm	March 1918. Batln in Billets, training	
	2nd-10th		Reinforcements arrived as follows: 5 Officers & 64 O. Ranks	
			Batln moved by Route March to ALBERT thence	
BEAULEN-	7th		train to BAPAUME & marched to Camp arrived 11:30 pm stay	
COURT	8th		C.O. with Offrs & NCOs to HERMIES vicinity to study	
			ground & wire views to counter attack	
	9th		Same party to HAYRINCOURT on a similar reconnaissance	
	11th		Similar party to LOUVERAL for the same purpose	
	8th-13th		Battn returned training & finally working parties on the	
			METZ defences	
	14th		Lt Col Q B Garrett left on leave for England, Major E Hawkes	
			assumed command of Battn.	
	15-20		Battn in Camp BEAULENCOURT	
	21	6am	Battn stand to	
		11:30	Battn struck camp at 12:30	

WAR DIARY or INTELLIGENCE SUMMARY

Army Form C. 2118.

Place	Date	Hour	Summary of Events and Information	Remarks and references to Appendices
SANDERS CAMP	21	12.30 pm	Batta. moved by march route to SANDERS CAMP. 3 casualties by shell fire en route.	
		5.30 pm	A Coy deputed rubs [?] move to "BEETROOT FACTORY" on the BAPAUME — CAMBRAI Road near LEBUCQUIERE to relieve 1 Company of Wiltshire in front line. Remainder of Batta. orders received to move to vicinity of "GRIKA COPSE" LE VELU and dig in in close support to counter attack prepared to be made by 57th & 58th Brigades. Batta. took position and acted.	
		11.30 pm	Orders received to withdraw Batta. from the position and moved by march route to vicinity of FREMICOURT.	
	22	3 am	Batta. arrived at FREMICOURT	
		8 am	Batta HQ moved Camp in FREMICOURT WOOD vacated by 57th Bn. HLI and Batta occupied Trench in East of the Wood being reserve Batt to K56 N of Bde who were in support in 55th Bde in defence of BEUGNY. Ground between FREMICOURT & BEUGNY reconnoitred by CO & OC 4 Companies.	

WAR DIARY or INTELLIGENCE SUMMARY

Army Form C. 2118.

Place	Date	Hour	Summary of Events and Information	Remarks and references to Appendices
	22nd March	11 a.m.	Battn. proceeded according to orders to vicinity of LEBUQIERE & taking up position in support of front line and consolidate. Coys. in position by 3 a.m. on 23rd	
	23	7.30 a.m.	S.O.S. put up by front line, repeated by Suffolks, no artillery response.	
		8.0 a.m.	Enemy reported to be advancing in large numbers against BAPAUME–CAMBRAI Road.	
		10.0 a.m. – 11 a.m.	25th Divn. seen to be withdrawing from across BAPAUME-CAMBRAI Rd. and forced through line held by Battn. Battn's Right flank left refused. Enemy seen crossing BAPAUME – CAMBRAI Road in large numbers, engaged at long range by heavies from A & B Coys. A Coy. having been withdrawn from fork by BEET ROOT FACTORY at 3.0 a.m. that morning.	
		11.0 a.m. – 1 p.m.	Large bodies of troops seen moving towards LE BUCQUIERE. Battn. HQ withdrawn to FREMICOURT – BEUGNY road & ordered to Coys. to withdraw fighting to GREEN LINE. Situation reported to Coy 9th Cheshires & GREEN LINE.	

WAR DIARY
or
INTELLIGENCE SUMMARY
(Erase heading not required.)

Army Form C. 2118.

Place	Date	Hour	Summary of Events and Information	Remarks and references to Appendices
		1.0 p.m	Both Battalions carried out successfully without heavy casualties & Battn. established in rear of 9th Cheshires & 6th N. Staffs on GREEN LINE	
		1.15 p.m	Attack from direction of BEUGNY seen developing and Battn ordered to withdraw to BANCOURT, & reorganise as Brigade Reserve.	
		3 p.m	W.K Manoeuvre completed. Battn. placed itself in readiness to move up to close support of the GREEN LINE. Battn. accommodated for the night in trenches in vicinity of BANCOURT.	
	about 10 a.m	Orders received from the C.O. of 6th N. Staffs for S.O.S. 8th Inf. Bde. to both move up Spartin Trenches in support of GREEN LINE	
		2.0 p.m	Major HAWKINS wounded and Capt HAZEL WOOD assumed command of Battn. Priests of Conference report to O.C. 8th N. Staffs	
		3.0 p.m	Instruction received that Lt Col. W.A. BOWEN V.D. had taken over command of the Battn.	
		4 P.M	Bn. was lettered by S.E. outskirts of BAPAUME & Coys holding in	
		10 P.M	Bn. ordered to take up line on BAPAUME - ALBERT Rd	

Army Form C. 2118.

WAR DIARY
or
INTELLIGENCE SUMMARY.
(Erase heading not required.)

Instructions regarding War Diaries and Intelligence Summaries are contained in F. S. Regs., Part II. and the Staff Manual respectively. Title pages will be prepared in manuscript.

Place	Date	Hour	Summary of Events and Information	Remarks and references to Appendices
	25th	8 AM	Bn on BAPAUME - ALBERT Rd. Took up Position of Obs on Opp. Delle Ros.	
		8.30AM	Rt Flank based until found to bridge N of Rd where Bn forward bt 11.30. Considerable heavy & innumerable enemy shorts about 4 Pts Rt Flank unshifted + 13= inches of WN toward Village GRAYVILLERS	
		3P.M	Bn left at my own to Cyl ground (W of IRLES Room on Rd between Cavy Rd Flank definitely exposed Bn inflicted losses at out Pts. + Got 14 men hurt W of MIRAMONT.	
		10PM	behind running fire good O.G. + 3 Pts left in outskirts of refuge of HEBUTERN	
	26th	9AM	Moved into HEBUTERN. Bn at church of village in SAILLY AU BOIS Pd + others in other army huts huts.	
		11AM	Bn left at bigh of HEBUTERN SAILLY Rd & Pd on 4 BM & Lines by Authorities Puits of 10 PM 6 bldrs + lived in SAILLY	
	27th		Day Spent in SAILLY	
	28th		Bn moved to FAMECHON total Uhr. for night	
	29th		Bn moved to CANDAS 12 miles & entrained for CHESTNS	

MVB DIVBN

WAR DIARY
or
INTELLIGENCE SUMMARY.

Army Form C. 2118.

Place	Date	Hour	Summary of Events and Information	Remarks and references to Appendices
	30⁻		Bn. arrive CAESTRE 1 AM & embuss for KEMMEL arriving in camp about 3 AM	
	31st		day spent in camp at KEMMEL.	

56th Brigade.
19th Division.

1/4th BATTALION

KING'S SHROPSHIRE LIGHT INFANTRY

APRIL 1918.

Army Form C. 2118.

1/4 Sherwood 56/79

WAR DIARY
or
INTELLIGENCE SUMMARY.
(Erase heading not required.)

WO 95/4415

9. R.
Gabet

Place	Date	Hour	Summary of Events and Information	Remarks and references to Appendices
	1/4/16		Batt. left KEMMEL and proceeded to GABLE CAMP by march route	
WULV- ERGHEM	2/4/16		Stood in GABLE CAMP - Training & refitting	
	6/4/16		Major WINGROVE joined as 2 i/c	

WAR DIARY or INTELLIGENCE SUMMARY

Army Form C. 2118.

Place	Date	Hour	Summary of Events and Information	Remarks and references to Appendices
WOLVERGHEM	19/4/18	5.30 am	Battn orders to stand by.	
		8.30	Battn orders to move & take up a new slope of Hill 63, in support of 7th Bn.	
		12 noon	Battn took up position on Hill 63. Two Coys forwards, one Coy in R. Gauk at Lindenhock Farm, one Coy in support. Heavy enemy shelling in 7th Brigade Barrage during move. 2 killed 4 wounded.	
HILL 63	11/4/18	2 pm	Enemy attacked Kemmel on right rear, our Coy and Bounets to remain to watch L. Res. movements.	
			Some Continuous Batt Bomb Barrage No. 90 at T.18 c.n.	
		6 pm	Major Risington took over from Col. Browne.	
		7.10	Heavy enemy barrage on Hill 63. Staff. Shropshires began to withdraw thro' our lines. Battn withdrew to Army Line in Ouvry Sime between position in Ouvry Line between	
ARMY LINE		9.0	WULVERGHEM – NEUVE EGLISE Rd & road at T.6 a 1.8.	
		11.0		

WAR DIARY
or
INTELLIGENCE SUMMARY.
(Erase heading not required.)

Army Form C. 2118.

Place	Date	Hour	Summary of Events and Information	Remarks and references to Appendices
Army Line	12/4/18	9.30	Day fairly quiet. Enemy attacks line driven off by rifle S.M.G. fire.	
	13/4/18	8.0 am	Small parties of enemy funtionis into NEUVE EGLISE were driven out by elements of K.S.L.I. – K.O.Y.L.I. – Y & L & R.E. armoures by 72nd M.G.	
		6.0 am	Barrage put down on line.	
		8.30 am	Orders received from 108th Inf. Bde. to take over ARMY LINE North of NEUVE EGLISE Rd Rees Ry to YL	
		9.45 am	movement carried out. Both H.Q. moved to barn in T9.D.97	
	14/4/18	9.0 am	line of N&S Road withdrawn to line running parallel to NEUVE EGLISE Rd. Enemy occupies part of NEUVE EGLISE village.	

Place	Date	Hour	Summary of Events and Information	Remarks and references to Appendices
ARMY LINE	14/4/18	2.0 am	Enemy heavily shelled by T.M.B.	
		6.0	Enemy withdrawn 1500yds N.W. of WOLVERGHEM - NEUVE EGLISE RD to entrance of NEUVE EGLISE.	
			From T.B. 9.6. to river line.	
		9.0	Major Livingstone wounded & Capt Ware killed.	
		9.30	Troops in line parallel to withdrawn positions.	
			NEUVE EGLISE orders to withdraw to ROSSIGNOL CAMP.	
	15/4/18	1.30 am	Remnants holding entrance & ensuing no troops on their left withdrawing to safety. Batn were orders to join Batn. at ROSSIGNOL CAMP.	
		8.30	Major MARTIN MC 6th N.S.R. assumes command of Batn.	

WAR DIARY
or
INTELLIGENCE SUMMARY.

Army Form C. 2118.

Place	Date	Hour	Summary of Events and Information	Remarks and references to Appendices
ROSSIGNOL CAMP	15/4/18	—	Battn reorganises, two parties on fatigue	
	19/4/18	10.40 am	Battn orders to take up position in reserve in N.30.A+B.	
N.30 A+B		11.40 am	Battn in position in N.30.A+B.	
		2.25 pm	Battn places under orders of 56th Bde.	
		6.20	Battn H.Q. moves N.14.c.9.3.	
		12 n't	Battn strength after 9 Offrs 394 OR's including 15 OR's attached from 56 T.M.B. H.Q. N.14.D.6.1.	
	19/4/18	1 pm	Operation orders for night by 38th Trench Du received	
	19/4/18	5.30	Orders to withdraw in accordance with O.O. received	
	19/4/18	4.33 am	withdrawal commenced	
	19/4/18	5.30 am	Withdrawal complete Battn rendezvous at Rossmore Down	
			Battn moves to Bernet at withdrawn by march route	

WAR DIARY
or
INTELLIGENCE SUMMARY.

(Erase heading not required.)

Army Form C. 2118.

Place	Date	Hour	Summary of Events and Information	Remarks and references to Appendices
WIPPENHOEK	20/4/18		Baths resting at WIPPENHOEK.	
	21/4/18	9 am	Batn. left by march route for TUNNELLER'S CAMP.	
TUNNELLER'S CAMP	22/4/18		Training and organization	
	23/4/18		— do —	
	24/4/18		— do —	
	25/4/18	10 pm	Left by march route to take up position of readiness at OUDROOM.	
OUDROOM	26/4/18		Moved up to position of readiness, frontline with road G.29.c.8.4. and X roads G.29.6. cm. (28.S.W.)	
	27/4		— do —	
	28/4		— do —	
	29/4		— do —	
	30/4/18		Position unchanged	

A.B. Brown
Lieut. Col. Commdg
1/4 K.S.L.I.

WAR DIARY
or
INTELLIGENCE SUMMARY.
(Erase heading not required.)

Army Form C. 2118.

1/4 H & L I
May 1918

Place	Date	Hour	Summary of Events and Information	Remarks and references to Appendices
OUDARDOM	1/5/18		Left OUDARDOM for sector held by elements of 18th Kings Yorkshire & 2nd Bedford Regt	(Nos 127-156 77 to M36 c48)
DICKEBUSCH	2/5/18		Bn HQ established @ H.36 c. Relieved Kings Yorkshire & Bedford Regt in front line	
"	3/5/18	4 PM	Relief complete Position of BnHQ changed to IRISH FARM H.36 c 05	
"	"		Destroyed German transport wagon	
"	4/5/18		Relieved by ARGYLE & SUTHERLANDS.	
N. BUSSEBOOM	5/5/18	1:30 AM	Relief complete Bn proceeded en route to N of BUSSEBOOM (CAMP 31 NW S.16 B.24)	
"	"	5 AM	Arrived BUSSEBOOM	
"	"	3:30 PM	Left BUSSEBOOM en route for camp at L-136 (J.72) 1200 ORs from transport lines	
"	"	7 PM	Arrived L.13 679 — joined by 4 Off & 1200 ORs	
L.13.6 (J.28)	6/5/18		Reorganisation & training	
"	7/5/18		do	standing to at ½ hours notice.
"	8/5/18		do	
"	9/5/18		do	
NEY DICKEBUSCH	10/5/18	Midday	Left by light railway for line to relieve 9th R Welsh F.	
"	11/5/18	3 AM	Relief complete 6 Bay suffered 9 casualties during relief	
"	"		Bn HQ H.24 C 66 (J.18)	
"	12/5/18	12 Mdnt	Relieved by Notts & Derby's Regt	
"	"		Relief complete. Bn proceeded by light railway to camp L.13. (G.27)	
L.13.6	13/5/18		On arrival	
"	14/5/18	4 PM	Reorganisation & training	
"	15/5/18			

Army Form C. 2118.

WAR DIARY
or
INTELLIGENCE SUMMARY.

(Erase heading not required.)

May 1918

Place	Date	Hour	Summary of Events and Information	Remarks and references to Appendices
L 13 b	16/5	11:30 pm	Proceeded by route march to WAAYENBORE	
	17/5	3:45 pm	Entrained for CHALONS	
OMEY	18/5	7 PM	Bn detrained at VETRY-LA-VILLE & marched to billets in OMEY	
	19/5		Re-organisation	
	20/5		Training	
	21/5		do	
	22/5		do	
	23/5		do	
	24/5		do	
	25/5		do	
	26/5		do	
	27/5		do	
	28/5	11/10 pm	Bn moved in motor buses under sealed orders	
※ M.CHAUMUZY	29/5	5:40 AM	Detrained on road & marched to billets (slaughterhouse)	※ SOISSONS 22.
		6.10	Arrived in billets	
		11.10	Moved from Slaughterhouse	
CHAMBRECY		12.40	Arrived at CHAMBRECY	
		4.40	Moved from " to take up position in line NNE of JARDY	
E of BOULEUSE	30 "	12.30	Bn in position holding line on ridge from ranged to wood. HQ in farm 1000 yds in rear. C & D Coys in line A Coy in support	
		11-0 AM	Enemy attacked after heavy bombardment. 2 platoons of A Coy sent forward to reinforce front line. Flanks forced to withdraw — 3 platoons remaining from A Coy sent back to cover own withdrawal	
		1 PM	Bn HQ moved	
		2 "	Bn ordered to withdraw to ridge E of AUBILLY. Bn reassembled. French holding the ridge.	

(89979) Wt W3355/P466 60,000 10/17 D. D. & L. Sch Bn. Forms/C2118/5.

Army Form C. 2118.

WAR DIARY
of
INTELLIGENCE SUMMARY.
(Erase heading not required.)

May/18 3rd Sheet

Instructions regarding War Diaries and Intelligence Summaries are contained in F. S. Regs., Part II. and the Staff Manual respectively. Title pages will be prepared in manuscript.

Place	Date	Hour	Summary of Events and Information	Remarks and references to Appendices
	30/5	4.0 PM	Bn Casualties approx 180 ? 6 officers.	
		6 PM	Boys fall up position on left of ridge	
		10 PM	Bn withdrew to take up position in support to French NW of BLIGNY	
	31/5	1 AM	Bn in position — HQ in bank N of BLIGNY	
			Lieut Col W.A. Brown in command of remainder of 9th Div. 30th Regt.	
		Noon	Bn moved up in close support to French	
			Bn HQ moved to lodge S of BLIGNY.	
			Enemy artillery active.	
		4 PM	Enemy attacked + French withdrew — Bn counter attacked & regained position.	
			Casualties approx 80 + 2 officers.	
		6	Situation quietened down. Enemy shelled bn HQ + troops on left — French 20th Regt on Right.	
			Great aerial activity.	

D.W. Brown Lt Col
Commg 1/4 K.S.L.I.

1/4 th Shrop. L.I.
5/19
June 1918

Army Form C. 2118.

INTELLIGENCE SUMMARY
(Erase heading not required)

Place	Date	Hour	Summary of Events and Information	Remarks and references to Appendices
Bridge E of BLIGNY	June 1	9.30am	Bn withdrew a little to take up new position. A Coy in touch with 23 Bde Coy on right & B Coy in touch with 1 troops on left.	
	2		Bn not moved to Slaughterhouse – Situation quiet.	
		12.30am	Enemy Patrols walked into our lines	
			Aeroplanes heavy active indentification dropped several bombs on the Bn lines. Situation very quiet.	
	3	10am	More bombs dropped – Situation unchanged	
	4	3.30 am	"B" Coy established advanced Gd post in advance of our front line. Enemy shelling very constant.	
CHAUMUZY			Bn HQ moved to CHAUMUZY	
	5	3-3.30am	Bn moved back into new CHAUMUZY line as Gurkha attack failure	
			Situation very quiet.	
	6	10am	Enemy started to bombard 2 pin Hills	
			Hart [?] on left attacked & failed to withdraw a little. Gurkha withdrew on right.	
		12.0m	Bn moves to retake position MONTAGNE or BLIGNY. Maj WARNFORD in charge of Battn	
		7.0 pm	attack MONTAGNE de BLIGNY started Battn reached in both flanks	
		1.45	During counter attack Battn scattered. D/o Comdr. wounded from Bn. Lieut Benjamin "C" Coy gained reputation.	
			Engl. Infantry on their way failed to attack. Casualties affairs 2 officers 70 ORs	
			Bn relieved by 56rx Canadian Bn.	
Bois de COURTON ?	7	4.0am	Bn arrived Bois de COURTON Bois reserve	
			Lt Col WH. Brown awarded DSO. Capt Bunker–Capt Haywood & Capt Fry MCs	
	9		QM RSM awarded MC. Lt Buckley "A"	
	10.		Bn from Res to Lt Buckley, Lt Thomas & Lt Davis to Brev de Conde for new line I Bligny	

WAR DIARY or INTELLIGENCE SUMMARY.

1/4 Kings Shropshire Light Infy

Army Form C. 2118.

Instructions regarding War Diaries and Intelligence Summaries are contained in F.S. Regs., Part II. and the Staff Manual respectively. Title pages will be prepared in manuscript.

(Erase heading not required)

Place	Date	Hour	Summary of Events and Information	Remarks and references to Appendices
Bois de Courton	10th		56th Bde formed into 56th Composite Bn — S.Staffs A Coy — KSLI B Coy — Cheshires C Coy	
			Capt Burke in charge of B Coy	
NW CHAUMUZY	11th		56th Bn went into line	
	12th	4:0AM	holding line NW of CHAUMUZY	
	13th		situation quiet	
	14th		B Coy back into Support	
	16		situation unchanged	
	17th		"	
	18th		56th Bn relieved by Italians	
HAUTVILLERS WOOD	19th		Bn reorganised into 1/4 KSLI	
	20th	5:30AM	proceeded by route march to LE MESNIL	
LE MESNIL		12:0AM	arrived LE MESNIL. to men fell out	15 miles
		3:20	2/D H Grans paraded with Brig. de Grens by French Lepol Bn	
	21st	5:20	moved by lorries to new area	
		9:0	arrived OYES	
OYES	22nd		Reorganisation & training	
	23		"	
BROUSSY Le PETIT	24	3:0PM	moved to BROUSSY Le PETIT	
		4:0	arrived	
	25		Reorganisation & training	
	26		"	
	27		"	
	28		"	
	29		"	
	30		"	

Wm de Brampton Rigg
Commanding 1/4 KSLI

1/4 Shropshire Army Form C2118
July 1918
Vol 13

12.R
2 sheet

WAR DIARY
INTELLIGENCE SUMMARY
(Erase heading not required)

Place	Date	Hour	Summary of Events and Information	Remarks and references to Appendices
BAUSSY la PETIT (?)	2nd	7.30pm	Training	
		1-0pm	Bn moved by route march to AULNAY aux PLANCHES	
AULDNAY aux PLANCHES		1.15	" Arrived @ AULDNAY aux PLANCHES	
	3rd	11.0	" in Billets	
		3.30	Bn marched to FERE-CHAMPANIES to entrain for new area	
		7.30pm	Detrained & railhead 2 coys A&B left behind to follow to next train	
AZINCOURT	4th	2.30am	Bn arrived @ AZINCOURT 7 went into billets	
	5th	3.40	Bathing	
	6th		Genl Conference afternoon	
VERCOUGH	7th	8.0	Bn marched to VERCOUGH	
		11.20	" arrived @ "	
	8th		Following unifrom & annual 2 officers 134 ORs	
	9		Training	
	10th		"	
	11		Following officers awarded M.C: Capt G.F. Fitzgerald — 2Lt H. Coben	
	12th		2/Lt D.O. Jordan. C.O. — 2/Lt H. GRAVES.	
	13th	9.0am	Bn moved by Busses to new area — LIE'RES	
LIERES		2.0pm	Bn arrived & marched into Billets	
	14		Training following uniform annual. 18 ORs	
	15		" " 16 ORs	
	16		" " 1 Officer	
	17		" " 5 ORs	
	18		" " 19 ORs	
	19		" " 4 ORs	
	20			

Army Form C. 2118.

WAR DIARY
or
INTELLIGENCE SUMMARY.
(Erase heading not required.)

July 1918

Place	Date	Hour	Summary of Events and Information	Remarks and references to Appendices
LIERES	26th		Batln training	
	22		"	
	23		"	
"	24		" Following reinforcement arrived 2 Officers	
	25		" " 2 ORs	
	26		" " 20 ORs	
	27		" "	
	28		" "	
	29		" "	
	30		" "	
	31		" "	

Lt. Bramford Major
Comdg 1/4 K.S.L.I

1/4 Sharp Army Form C. 2118
13 R
2 sheet

WAR DIARY
INTELLIGENCE SUMMARY
August 1918

(Erase heading not required.)

16

Place	Date	Hour	Summary of Events and Information	Remarks and references to Appendices
LIÉRES	Aug 1st		Training	
	2		"	
	3		"	
	4		"	
	5		"	
	6	12.30 A	Bn Embussed for LA BOUVERIE	
		4.45	Debussed LA BOUVERIE & marched to BOUVERIE	
		9.30	Bn proceeded to line to relieve 9th K.S.L.I. in support	
LA BASSEE CANAL	7th	11.55	Relief complete. A Coy holding INVERNESS line B & D PERTH line HQ on canal bank, W.23.c.9.4.	
H 26 A&E	8		Bn in training trenches	
	9		A & C Coys moved forward to ABERDEEN line from B Coy having advanced 100x into LOCON.	
	10		Relieved B & D Coys in front line	
LOCON	11th	12.50 pm	Relief complete A & B Coys holding front line to an support D coys in EDINBORO support line	
			H.Q. X.13.D.20.	
	12		Improving positions	
		10.15pm	2 Canada officers seen going into house 50x in front of A Coys front post NW CRAMOND N. with some slaves garments & rifle grenades went forward. Obs? him & obtained very valuable information. Effectively clear forward of Blockhouse under 2/Lt PARKER to obtain touch with enemy. Stay encountered	
	13th	11.0pm	8 Coy being increased & being encountered to make clear the location in front. They advanced 100x & met with stubborn resistance by enemy M.C. fire 2nd Lt. H. MERINDON took some of his platoon forward to a house where enemy M.G. was believed to be emplaced. & captured & occupied in possession & the M.C.	
	14th	11.0 pm	D & C coys relieved A & B. improving positions	
	15			
	16th	11.0	Bn being relieved by 9th CHESHIRE Rgt	
	17	1.0	Relief complete about 70 casualties suffered during tour.	
ANNEZIN		3.15	Bn in FILLIES in ANNEZIN	

Army Form C. 2118.

WAR DIARY
or
INTELLIGENCE SUMMARY.
(Erase heading not required.)

Place	Date	Hour	Summary of Events and Information	Remarks and references to Appendices
ANNEZIN	18		Bns opening & cleaning u/o training	
	19			
	20			
	21	9-0am	Moved forward to support – 3 Coys took up positions and in front of canal. A Coy in reserve.	
	22	12-10p.	HQ took over from 2nd WORCESTER	
	23		Infantry trenches	
	24		"	
	25	9.0am	Bn started to move up to take over from 8th R. Staffs in front line.	
		12.0	Relief W.R. @ X18.S.10 Coys holding line to in relieve D on left joined with 1 Gloucesters on right. 3 Coys.	
	26		Hard day doing trench patrols	
		8.30	Bn JHQ moved to X.1.2.9.3.	
	27	night	Coys changed over. A in support B in reserve	
	28	8.0	2/LT SHELDON & his platoon came up from reserve to raid enemy positions	
		9.40	5 Enemy T/ M.E captured – front coys moved outpost forward 300x	
	29	7-0pm	Patrols still advancing Right patrol of D coy entered NEUVE CHAPELLE	
		8.15p	Reserve Coy (B) moved forward 500x occupying D Coy former positions	
			Bn being relieved by ROYAL WARWICKSHIRE Regt.	
	30	1-0am	Relief complete	
			Bn moved back to CHOCQUES by light railway	
		2.30am	Bn in billets	
	31	"	Reorganising training	

M Bonner J.M. Tony. 4/KSLI.

4/ Shropshire L.I.
95/70

14 R.
3 sheets

WAR DIARY
of
INTELLIGENCE SUMMARY
(Erase heading not required)

Army Form C. 2118.

September 1918. VII/15

Place	Date	Hour	Summary of Events and Information	Remarks and references to Appendices
CHOQUES	1		Training	
	2		"	
	3		"	
	4		Batt. awarded "Croix de Guerre et Palme" for operations at BLIGNY. June 6. 1918.	
			Batt. ordered to relieve 5th Brigade in front of VIEILLE CHAPELLE	
		3.15 pm	Relief cancelled owing to enemy withdrawal	
LE TOURET.	5	1.30 pm	Entrained on L.R. for LE TOURET.	
		5.50	Batt. detrained LE TOURET.	
			Batt. relieved 9th Shamrocks Division (47th Div.) in line of retention	
	6		N of RICHBOURG ST VAAST.	
			Line of retention moved forward in front of RICHBOURG ST VAAST	
	7		Consolidating line of retention	
	8		-do-	
E BOIS BIEZ	9	7 do Batt moved forward to relieve 9th Cheshires (Left Batt. of 1st BRIGADE)		
			6 pm Coy in front line at B in support Batt HQ Edward's Post. Active Patrols.	
	10	12.45 am	Relief complete	

Army Form C. 2118.

WAR DIARY
of
INTELLIGENCE SUMMARY.
(Erase heading not required.)

September 1918

Instructions regarding War Diaries and Intelligence Summaries are contained in F. S. Regs., Part II. and the Staff Manual respectively. Title pages will be prepared in manuscript.

Place	Date	Hour	Summary of Events and Information	Remarks and references to Appendices
E. BOIS GRENIER	10		Weather bad. Consolidating trenches. Active patrolling at night.	
	11		– do –	– do –
	12		– do –	– do –
	13	2.15am	Inter-Coy relief. B relieved C on left. A relieved D on right.	
	14	9.30pm	A Coy relief complete. Active patrolling.	
	15		A Coy advance their line 100 yards in minor operation	
	16		A Coy consolidating new position	
LOCON	17	1am	Batt relieved by 3rd Worcestrs. moved to LOCON by L.R.	
	18th	4.30am	Batt in Camp.	
			Cleaning up	
	19th		Cleaning up & reorganisation	
	20th		TRAINING	
	21st	5am	Batt left LOCON & marched to relieve the 2nd WILTS Regt.	PIETRE Listo...
			Batt H.Q. M.28.d.9.2.)	
CRICETA		11.30am	Relief complete. A & B Coy in support in B. Line, C & D Coy	
			in out Post line	

Army Form C. 2118.

WAR DIARY
or
INTELLIGENCE SUMMARY.
(Erase heading not required.)

September 1918.

Place	Date	Hour	Summary of Events and Information	Remarks and references to Appendices
CRICHETH	22.		A & B Coy improving B line. C & A Coy very active patrolling steaming enemy wire in front of MAUDELINE TRENCH which was being cut by artillery with a view to attack.	
	23		— do —	
	24.		— do — Although artillery claimed wire cut no defined gaps could be seen by patrols.	
	25		Active patrolling claimed consolidation of front & trying to ascertain strength of posts at LA MOTTES FERME & PIERRE MILL	
	26.	10 pm	Inter Coy relief. B relieves A Coy relieves C Coy.	
	27	2 am	Relief complete. Active patrolling.	
	28		All Coys improving their line. Active patrols to ascertain strength of posts at LES MOTTES FERME, PIERRE MILL & N.36.c.2.9	PIERRE 1:10000
	29th	3 am	Final conference all Coy commanders & Platoon Commanders at Bn HQ M.28.d.9.2.	"
	30.	1.30am	C & D Coys move to jumping off spots. A & B move to support positions	"
		4.30am	All Coys in position ready to go forward.	
		7.30am	Attacked Les LAIES DITCH + patrol pushed out when 2/Lt of Ditch. All objectives gained. 2.45am. 2/Lieuts HARTY & LEACH killed	"
			2/Lt MARRINDEN dangerously wounded.	
		6 pm	NOTION TRENCH successful attacked & dark established at junction of NOTION & DORA TRENCH.	
		10.30pm	RHF relieved by 8th N Staffs	

WAR DIARY
or
INTELLIGENCE SUMMARY
(Erase heading not required.)

Army Form C. 2118.

S/19/4 Sheet L1
Vol 16

Place	Date	Hour	Summary of Events and Information	Remarks and references to Appendices
LACOUTRE	1st	22.30	Batt relieved by 8th N.S. from Le LAIES DITCH. Marched to Kinchin in front of LACOUTRE. Relief incomplete No.7 platoon still in the line.	Trench Map
	2nd	05.00	Relief by 8th N.S. complete.	
			Batt relieved by 15th R.W.F. but had to take this batt. to the "B" Line owing to German withdrawal over AUBERS RIDGE	
		12.00	Relief complete.	
		18.00	Batt entrained on Light Railway for BUR-BUR.	
	3	03.60	Arrived BUR-BUR marched CHAMBLAIN CHATELAIN	
CHAMBLAIN-CHATELAIN		04.00	Batt in billets. Cleaning up.	
	4		Cleaning up.	
		15.00	Batt entrained CALONNE RIQUART. arrived at SAULTY STATION at 23.00.	LENS 11
BAVINCOURT	5	01.00	marched to BAVINCOURT.	
			Billets in BAVINCOURT. Cleaning up.	
	6		TRAINING.	
	7	17.30	Batt embussed at SAULTY STATION for GRAINCOURT	Sheet
GRAINCOURT		19.30	Marched to bivouacs between MEOUVRES + GRAINCOURT	57c NE 8th Bn Local
		21.30	Batt bivouaced	

Army Form C. 2118.

WAR DIARY
or
INTELLIGENCE SUMMARY

(Erase heading not required.)

Instructions regarding War Diaries and Intelligence Summaries are contained in F. S. Regs., Part II. and the Staff Manual respectively. Title Pages will be prepared in manuscript.

Place	Date	Hour	Summary of Events and Information	Remarks and references to Appendices
GRAINCOURT	8th		Training	
	9	11.00	Batt. moved to a camp in square E.29.- T.5. at 14.00. Billeting over from. 8th Gloucester Regt. Batt. in camp at 15.00	Sheet 57.c
PROVILLE	10	15.00	Batt. moved for PROVILLE. Arrived at PROVILLE men had to clean out billets, as they were left in evacuated by the enemy. Parties sent out cleaning up the roads, collecting dead from the roads for burial.	Sheet 57 b.
	11		Cleaning up battlefield area.	
	12	08.30 09.30	Training. Cleaning up battlefield area.	
		16.30 18.00	Batt. moved to take over billets vacated by 8th Gloucesters HQ. A.22.b.8.7. Batt. billeted	Sheet 57 b NN
CAMBRAI	13	08.45 10.30	TRAINING. CHURCH PARADE. Scouts supplied guard of honour to the FRENCH PREMIER.	
	14/15/16		Training	
	17	12.00	Batt. moved across country as an advanced guard forward to AVESNES [LEZ AUBERT] arriving in	Sheet 51/SW

Army Form C. 2118.

WAR DIARY
or
INTELLIGENCE SUMMARY
(Erase heading not required.)

Instructions regarding War Diaries and Intelligence Summaries are contained in F. S. Regs., Part II. and the Staff Manual respectively. Title Pages will be prepared in manuscript.

Place	Date	Hour	Summary of Events and Information	Remarks and references to Appendices
YESNES LEZ AUBERT	18		TRAINING	Sheet
	19	20:00	Batt moved into # Arrival raein at Y.19 central	51 A SE
	20	09:15	Batt moved further forward still in reserve at V.14 central.	Sheet
ST. AUBERT		10:00	arrived in billets in ST AUBERT.	51 A SE
	21		Cleaning up billets	
	22		TRAINING	
	23	0.900	Batt. moved across country as an advanced guard, until H.S toffs reconnoitring an enemy, proceeded	Sheet
			to CAGNONCLES.	51 A S.W.
CAGNONCLES	24	14:00	Arrived in Billets	
		09:00	TRAINING	
ST. AUBERT	25	14:00	Batt moved across Country # proceeded to ST AUBERT.	
		17:00	Arrived in billets.	
	26	10:00	Batt. standing by under 1 hours notice to move forward.	
		10:00	Batt. moved across country to CAGNONCLES.	
CAGNONCLES	27	13:00	Arrived in billets	
	28	10:30	Church Parade	
	29 30		TRAINING	
CAGNONCLES	31		-- " --	

WAR DIARY or INTELLIGENCE SUMMARY

Army Form C. 2118.

4/Sherwood F.
November 1918

16 R
5 sheet

Place	Date	Hour	Summary of Events and Information	Remarks and references to Appendices
CAGNONCLES	1	07:30	Batt moved across country to VENDEGIES, it halted from	Vol. 12
		11:45 – 14:15	at HAUSSY	
VENDEGIES	2	15:45	Batt. moved to MARESCHES and took up position NE of the village	
	3		Batt. advanced to high ground S.W. of JENLAIN, during the afternoon of this day, the battalion came under heavy shell fire, & had to advance under constant machine gun fire	
JENLAIN	4	06:00	Batt attacked through JENLAIN + on arriving E of JENLAIN manoeuvred many casualties (10). The Bn consolidated on a line running N from Warfurie. Le Grand Bn Station. Capt Jordan was killed & Lieuts Ox (Cheshire) attached F.S.I. was severely wounded.	
MARGNIES LE-GRAND	5	06:45	Batt passed through to 8 R. Staffs at this hour + continued the attack to LE CALOTIN with slight casualties. Held up for 3 hours only, units on flank not keeping up, continued attack and consolidated on high ground E of LA FLAMENGRIE. One casualty. Large supply of A.B. Cogs (the advance guard at remnants of Bettrechies + reports making stolen A table in place 2nd 6 inches of th deck bridge lowered to precipitate a night crossing	
LA FLAMENGRIE	6			

Army Form C. 2118.

WAR DIARY
or
INTELLIGENCE SUMMARY
(Erase heading not required.)

Instructions regarding War Diaries and Intelligence Summaries are contained in F.S. Regs., Part II. and the Staff Manual respectively. Title Pages will be prepared in manuscript.

Place	Date	Hour	Summary of Events and Information	Remarks and references to Appendices
LA FLAMENGRIE	6		The battalion relieved during the night 6-7 by the Worcester Regt. & marched to billets on the morning of the 7th. During the night of the 6th two shells fell outside BHQ at BRY & caused casualties to 1 officer and 8 O.R. Lt Hibberd was killed & 2 men of the advance party were killed and 6 wounded – this was most regrettable as they were the last casualties up to cessation of hostilities	Vol.12.
BRY	7			
BRY	8	09.00	Owing to exigence of situation caused by rapid retirement of enemy, the Batt. compelled to march to TAISNIERES via LA FLAMENGRIE & HOUDAIN. Men very weary & footsore but the march was completed under trying circumstances without a man falling out. Billeted at TAISNIERES & heard that the enemy had departed at 06.00 the same day by R.	
TAISNIERES	9		Batt. sent out reconnaissance patrol to BOIS DE LA LANIERE & report no sign of enemy, our cavalry patrol went that The enemy have retired beyond Railway running N & S through BOIS DE LANIERE.	
AISNIERES	10	0930	Batt. marched to BRY via HOUDAIN & BETTRICHES & halted at the	

Army Form C. 2118.

WAR DIARY
or
INTELLIGENCE SUMMARY
(Erase heading not required.)

Instructions regarding War Diaries and Intelligence Summaries are contained in F. S. Regs., Part II. and the Staff Manual respectively. Title Pages will be prepared in manuscript.

Place	Date	Hour	Summary of Events and Information	Remarks and references to Appendices
HOUDAIN	10	1030	at the former village to pick up packs & blankets. Progress very slow owing to congestion of traffic caused by destruction of bridge at BETTRICHES. Arrived at BRY at 16.00 & batt. billeted.	Val 12
BRY	11		Batt. cleaning up. At 09.30 received official intimation of cessation of hostilities at 11.00, at which hour the band played the French & British national anthems in the square. All the troops excited. All def. received.	
BRY	12		General cleaning of arms, equipment, billets being checked.	
	13		Batt. calming from battle area.	
VENDIGIES	14	0915	Batt. marched to VENDIGIES. arrived in billets at 15.00	
RIEUX	15	0845	Batt. marched to RIEUX arrived in billets at 13.00.	
	16		General cleaning up.	
	17		CHURCH PARADES.	
	18	0915 1130 1400 15.30	TRAINING + BATHS. Recreational training	

Army Form C. 2118.

WAR DIARY
or
INTELLIGENCE SUMMARY
(Erase heading not required.)

Instructions regarding War Diaries and Intelligence Summaries are contained in F. S. Regs., Part II. and the Staff Manual respectively. Title Pages will be prepared in manuscript.

Place	Date	Hour	Summary of Events and Information	Remarks and references to Appendices
RIEUX	19.	0900	TRAINING + BATHS.	
		1130		
		1400	Recreational TRAINING.	
		1530		
		1800	Concert given by 5th Field Ambulance.	
		2000		
	20	0930	Route MARCH.	
		1230		
		1400	Recreational TRAINING.	
		1530		
	21	0900	TRAINING + BATHS.	
		1130		
		1400	Recreational TRAINING.	
		15.30		
	22	0900	TRAINING	
		1130		
		1400	Recreational TRAINING.	
		1530		
	23.	0900	TRAINING	
		1130		
		1400	Recreational TRAINING	
		1530		

Army Form C. 2118.

WAR DIARY
or
INTELLIGENCE SUMMARY

(Erase heading not required.)

Instructions regarding War Diaries and Intelligence
Summaries are contained in F. S. Regs., Part II.
and the Staff Manual respectively. Title Pages
will be prepared in manuscript.

Place	Date	Hour	Summary of Events and Information	Remarks and references to Appendices
RIEUX	24th		Batt. moved by march route to CAMBRAI.	
CAMBRAI	25		Pulletta in southern outskirts of Cambrai.	
	26		" " "	
	27		" " "	
	28		Moved by bus to Rubempré	
RUBEMPRÉ	29		Training	
	30	0900	TRAINING.	
		1200		
		1400	Beneficial Training	
		1600		

Army Form C. 2118.

WAR DIARY or INTELLIGENCE SUMMARY

4/K.S.L.I.

(Erase heading not required.)

Place	Date	Hour	Summary of Events and Information	Remarks and references to Appendices
RU'BEMPRE	1.	morning / aft.	CHURCH PARADES. Recreational training	
	2.	0900 / 11:30	Training	
		14:00 / 15:30	Recreational training. About 50 Officers N.C.O.s & men attended lecture at NAOURS on Demobilization.	
	3.	0900 / 11:30	TRAINING.	
		14:00 / 15:30	Recreational Training	
	4.	09:00 / 11:30	TRAINING.	
		14:00 / 15:30	Recreational training. About 50 Officers & men attended lecture at NAOURS on "Bolshevism".	
	5.	0900	Route march 09:00 hrs to 12:30 hrs.	
	6.	09:00 / 9:15	Route march 09:00 hrs 15 Booths. Lecture by M.O. Subject ? Sick Reinforcement Officer joins Batn.	
	7.	09:00	Training.	

WAR DIARY or INTELLIGENCE SUMMARY

Army Form C. 2118.

Place	Date	Hour	Summary of Events and Information	Remarks and references to Appendices
RUMBEMPRÉ	8	09.40	Church Parade.	
		10.15	Lecture to Officers. "Beneath Fog Run".	
		11.30	Inspection of billets.	
	9	09.00	C.O. 4th reinforcements joined the Battn.	
		14.00	Coy Officer's inspection (A.F.B.213). Baths under Bay arrangements.	
	10	09.00	Bay Off's inspection (cut Boys)	
	11	09.10	Canadu – Route for Reconnoitring van Colour practices.	
		10.30	Lectures at TALMAS.	
	12	09.00	Reccr for Colour etc., Inclusive Remounts training	
	13	09.00	Move by march route to new area. Stages at MONTRELET & FIEFFES.	
FIEFFES & MONTRELET	14	08.30	Move by march route to VILLIERS L'HOPITAL. Arrived 14.00 p.m.	
VILLIERS L'HOPITAL	15	10.30	Church Parade.	
		11.30	Bay Off's inspection of billets	
	16	09.00	Bn on cleaning up and improvement of billets.	
		14.00	Colours (Regtl Kings) taken over from vacant; One Officer underwent joins Battn.	

Place	Date	Hour	Summary of Events and Information	Remarks and references to Appendices
VILLERS L'HOPITAL	17	09.00	Bn at Baths all day.	
	18	09.00	Training. Working parties on trench improvement. Lt. Col. Johnston assumes duties of 2 i/c Officer.	
	19	09.00 14.00	Sanctification Parade. Remainder — Parade – training. Working parties as for yesterday. On duty Bn.	
	20	09.00	Training. Working Parties as for yesterday. Bde guard mountings	
	21	09.15	Training. Working Parties as for yesterday. Major O/C & some Officers attend Lewis Gun instructions course to their own Regts.	
	22	09.30	On duty Battn. Church Parade.	
	23	09.00	An Officer joins Battn, now posted from 1st Regt. Training as per programme.	
	24	09.00	Bn at Baths. 200231 Pte Davis S. awarded Militia Militia	

WAR DIARY
or
INTELLIGENCE SUMMARY
(Erase heading not required.)

Army Form C. 2118.

Place	Date	Hour	Summary of Events and Information	Remarks and references to Appendices
VILLERS L'HOPITAL	25		Shut as Xmas Day.	
	26		Boxing Day — No parades.	
	27	09.00	Parades as per Programme — Training. Lt. Statham awarded M.C.	
	28	09.00	Parades as per Programme — Training	
	29	09.00	Church Parade.	
	30	09.00	Lieut Col "Jodrinis" Remainder Training. Major J.T. Tynan D.S.O. joins Battn, assumes command vice Lt Col "Brandon"	
	31	09.00	Lieut Col "Jodrinis" Remainder Training.	

J. Tynan Major
Cdg 1/4. K.S.L.I.

11/3 January 1919 **WAR DIARY** 4/Shropshire Army Form C. 2118
or
INTELLIGENCE SUMMARY
(Erase heading not required.)

YA 19

18 R
3 sheets

Place	Date	Hour	Summary of Events and Information	Remarks and references to Appendices
VIEUX 2/HOPITAL	1	9.0	Parades as per programme — Training	
	2+3		Parades as per programme — do	
	4			
	5	10.10	Lecture by Mr Hugh Brennan — Post War construction of Russia	
	6		Church Parade Bn in duty Bn	
	7		Training Parades	
	8		Training Parades	
	9		2 Coys Battn. and other 2 Training Bn in duty Bn.	
	10		2 Coys Battn. other two Training Brigade Rehearsal of Ceremonial in connection with the consecration of Colours for 5 N Staffs & 9 Cheshires.	
	11		Inter Coy. Cross country run. Weekly inspection Bn is duty Bn.	
	12		Church Parade	
	13		Parades as per programme — Training Second B.G. Rehearsal of Ceremonial. Bn is duty Bn	
	14 15		Parades as usual	

WAR DIARY
or
INTELLIGENCE SUMMARY
(Erase heading not required.)

Army Form C. 2118.

Place	Date	Hour	Summary of Events and Information	Remarks and references to Appendices.
VILLERS L'HOPITAL	16	9	3rd Bde. Rehearsal of ceremonial to shown by Lt. Col. RAYMER D.S.O.	
		1100	Lt-Col. B. Cronulow returned from leave	
	17.		Training Parades as per programme	
	18.		Bn is duty Bn.	
	19.		weekly inspection Church Parade.	
	20	9	4th Bde Rehearsal of ceremonial	
	21		Smartening up Drill.	
	22		Battln.	
	23		An audit board held to audit Canteen, C.O's + Band a/c.	
	24		Parades as per programme.	
	25			
	26		Church Parade. Bn is duty Bn.	
	27		Parades as per programme.	

Army Form C. 2118.

WAR DIARY
or
INTELLIGENCE SUMMARY

1/4 Shropshire L I

(Erase heading not required.)

Instructions regarding War Diaries and Intelligence Summaries are contained in F. S. Regs., Part II. and the Staff Manual respectively. Title Pages will be prepared in manuscript.

Place	Date	Hour	Summary of Events and Information	Remarks and references to Appendices
VILLERS L'HOPITAL	28		Rehearsal of Bde Concurial. all Iron Rations handed in	
	29.		Bn. Baths and Training	
	30		Bn. in duty Bn. Rehearsal of Bde Concurial. Played 1st K.S.L.9. at football at Authie	
	31.		Parades as per programme.	

JAS Combes
LT. COL.
COMDG. 1/4th BN. THE KINGS (SHROPSHIRE L.I.)

Army Form C. 2118.

1/4th Kings Shropshire Light Infy

9/11/20

WAR DIARY
or
INTELLIGENCE SUMMARY
(Erase heading not required.)

19.R.
2 sheets

Place	Date	Hour	Summary of Events and Information	Remarks and references to Appendices
BILLETS	1-2-19		TRAINING as per Programme. 19 OR demobilised	
	2		Church Parade. 23 " "	
	3		TRAINING as per Programme. 23 " "	
	4		Companies re-organised on two Platoon basis	
	5		BATT'N - Batt'n to study battalion 23 OR demobilised	
	6		TRAINING as per programme. 17 " "	
	7		" " " "	
	8		Battalion to study battalion	
	9		Church Parade.	
HOPITAL	10		PRINCE of WALES inspected the battalion when was present when the 9th Chinese Regt + 5th N. Staffordshire Regt were presented with their Colours by The PRINCE.	
	11		Training as per programme. 22 OR demobilised	
	12		Battalion to study Battalion 16 " "	
	13		ROUTE MARCH. " "	
	14		TRAINING as per programme.	
	15		Battalion to study battalion R.S.M. Wilson + 12 OR demobilised	
	16		CHURCH Parade. 18 OR demobilised	
	17		Educational Training	
	18		Training as per programme.	
	19		Route March.	
	20		Battalion to study Battalion	

WAR DIARY
or
INTELLIGENCE SUMMARY
(Erase heading not required.)

Army Form C. 2118.

Place	Date	Hour	Summary of Events and Information	Remarks and references to Appendices
VILLERS	21		Battalion moved to billets occupied by 9th Cheshire Regiment. Lt Col. K.F. BROMILOW demobilised. Major J.J. Tynan assumes	3rd OR demobilised
L'HOPITAL	22		Training as per programme. Command of the Battalion	
	23		Church Parade.	
	24		Training as per programme.	
	25		Battalion v Duty Battalion Recreational training	
	26		Route March.	
	27			
	28		BATHS. Training as per programme. 17 OR Demobilised.	

W.T.Minster
CAPT.
1/4th BN. THE KINGS (SHROPSHIRE L.I.)

Army Form C. 2118.

1/4K Y.S.L.1

WAR DIARY
or
INTELLIGENCE SUMMARY
(Erase heading not required.)

MARCH 1919

Vol 21 (Peace dispersal)

Place	Date	Hour	Summary of Events and Information	Remarks and references to Appendices
VILLERS L'HOPITAL	March 1st		CQM Sgt WILLIAMS awarded MILITARY MEDAL by Army Commander	
	2nd		Training as per programme	
	3			
	4		10 Officers & 270 ORs of 4th Bn to join 6th Leinster Reg.	
	5		Parades as per programme	
	6		" " "	
	7			
	8			
	9			
	10		Moving up camp.	
	11			
	12		Surplus Stores & Transport moved to CANDAS	
	13		Parades as per Programme	
	14		do	
	15		do	
	16		do	
	17		do	
	18		do	
	19		do	
	20		do	
	21		do	
	22nd		MAJOR W.W. RENTOUL. M.C. assumes command of the Bn vice Lt Col. J.J. TYNAN D.S.O. handed over to O/C Royal Inniskilling Fusiliers.	

Army Form C. 2118.

WAR DIARY
or
INTELLIGENCE SUMMARY

(Erase heading not required.)

MARCH, 1919.

Instructions regarding War Diaries and Intelligence Summaries are contained in F.S. Regs., Part II. and the Staff Manual respectively. Title Pages will be prepared in manuscript.

Place	Date	Hour	Summary of Events and Information	Remarks and references to Appendices
	23		Parades as per Programme.	
	24		do	
	25		do do	
	26		do do	
	27		do do	
	28		do do	
	29		do do	
	30		do do	
	31		do do	

Army Form C. 2118.

WAR DIARY
or
INTELLIGENCE SUMMARY
(Erase heading not required.)

1/4 Bn R. (Ghlinghm R.l.)

98 23 Ceased

21 R
2 sheets

Place	Date	Hour	Summary of Events and Information	Remarks and references to Appendices
VILLERS au FLOS	May 1919 1	.	Working Party furnished for Range at Villers l'Hôpital.	
	2	.	— ditto —	
	3	.	Strength of unit on this date 15 Officers & 9 OR. (including attached) Parade of whole Bn.	
	4	.	Divine Service. Orders rec'd to reduce same to 3 Officers & 35 OR.	
	5	.	Major White Hadow MC proceeded on leave to UK. Sgt W. Atkinson assumes Working Party furnished for work on Range command in same.	
	6	.	R.Q.M. Sgt proceeded on leave (Special) to U/K. 2 Other Ranks left unit for Demobilization.	
	7	.	Working Party furnished for Range.	
	8	.	" "	
	9	.	" "	
	10	.	Lt. W.F. Beaty & 9 OR. left unit for Demobilization. 4 Officers left unit for attachment to R.G.A. Battery ex G Furnace.	
	11	.	Divine Service — Farewell address by Lt. 19? Dm Shrive.	
	12	.	Orders received for same to entrain at SAVY on 14.5.19.	
	13	.	Working party furnished at SAVOY. Programme made & arrangements for entraining.	
	14	.	Same leave Villers L'Hôpital for SAVOY & entrain.	

Army Form C. 2118.

WAR DIARY
or
INTELLIGENCE SUMMARY
(Erase heading not required.)

Place	Date	Hour	Summary of Events and Information	Remarks and references to Appendices
HAVRE	15 May 1919	—	Entrained at 07.00 hrs. Vehicles entrained at 07.00 hrs. Entrainment sent to No. 2 Embarkation Camp to await Embarkation.	
HARFLEUR	16	—	Later awaiting Embarkation.	
"	17	—	" "	
"	18	—	Later Embarked for Southampton.	

15/5/19

A. H. Kendal
Major
O/c. 14 Bn. R.S.F.

www.ingramcontent.com/pod-product-compliance
Lightning Source LLC
Chambersburg PA
CBHW081453160426
43193CB00013B/2470